STAR WARS®

CLONE WARS
ADVENTURES
VOLUME 10

designers
Darin Fabrick

assistant editor
Dave Marshall

editor
Jeremy Barlow

publisher
Mike Richardson

special thanks to Elaine Mederer, Jann Moorhead,
David Anderman, Leland Chee, Sue Rostoni, and
Carol Roeder at Lucas Licensing

The events in these stories take place sometime
during the Clone Wars.

www.titanbooks.com
www.starwars.com

STAR WARS: CLONE WARS ADVENTURES Volume 10, March 2008. Published by Titan
Books, a division of Titan Publishing Group Ltd., 144 Southwark Street, London SE1 0UP. Star
Wars © 2008 Lucasfilm Ltd. & ™. All rights reserved. Used under authorization. Text and
illustrations for Star Wars are © 2008 Lucasfilm Ltd. No portion of this publication may be
reproduced or transmitted, in any form or by any means, without the express written permission
of the copyright holder. Names, characters, places, and incidents featured in this publication either
are the product of the author's imagination or are used fictitiously. Any resemblance to actual
persons (living or dead), events, institutions, or locales, without satiric intent, is coincidental.
Printed in China

STAR WARS

CLONE WARS
ADVENTURES
VOLUME 10

"GRADUATION DAY"
script **Chris Avellone**
art **Stewart McKenny**
colors **Ronda Pattison**

"THUNDER ROAD"
script and art **The Fillbach Brothers**
colors **Pamela Rambo**

"CHAIN OF COMMAND"
script **Jason Hall**
art **Ethen Beavers**
colors **Dan Jackson**

"WAITING"
script and art **The Fillbach Brothers**
colors **Tony Avina**

lettering
Michael Heisler

cover
The Fillbach Brothers and Dan Jackson

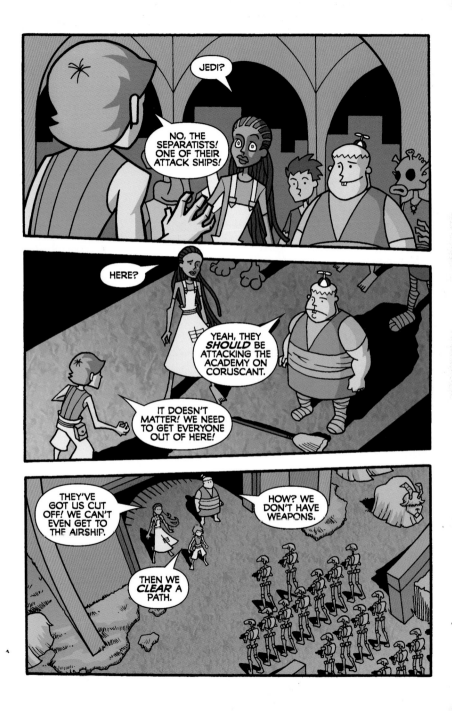

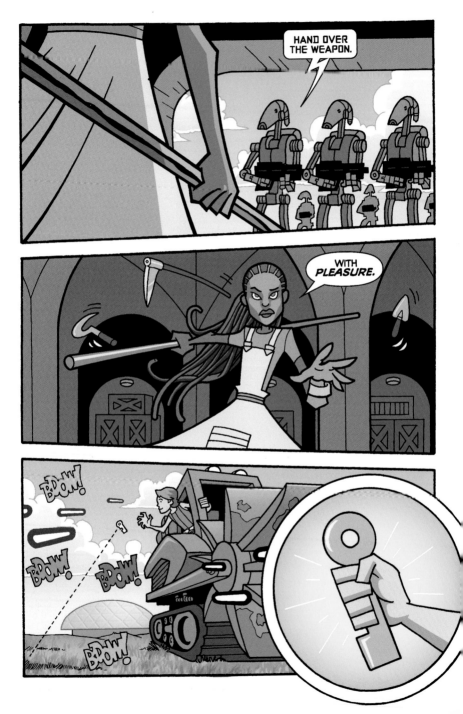

"...SACRIFICE IS A JEDI TRAIT...

BTEW BTEW BTEW BTEW BTEW BTEW BTEW

"...BUT WE DO *NOT* ABANDON OUR OWN."

THEY CAN HIDE ALL THEY WANT, BUT THERE'S ONLY *ONE* WAY OUT OF *DEATH CANYON...*

...THE THUNDER ROAD.

WHY'S IT CALLED THAT, *EH,* MOONEY?

IN A PLACE CALLED *"DEATH CANYON"* THEY JUST COULDN'T CALL IT *"FLOWER ROAD,"* NOW, COULD THEY?

SHUT UP, YOU TWO! COME ON, WE'LL HEAD THEM OFF AT THE PASS.

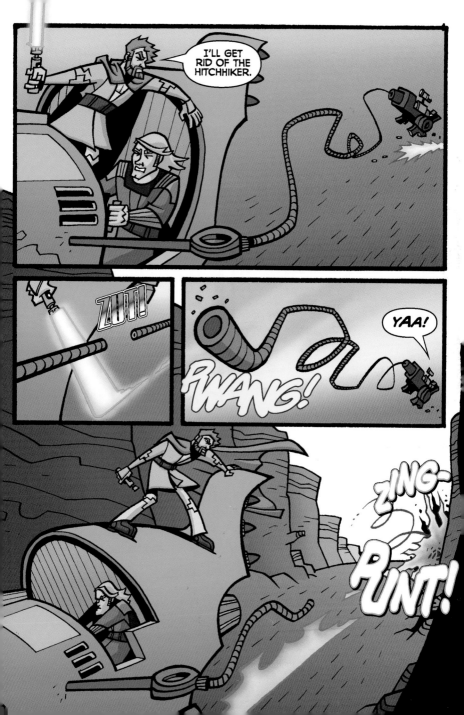

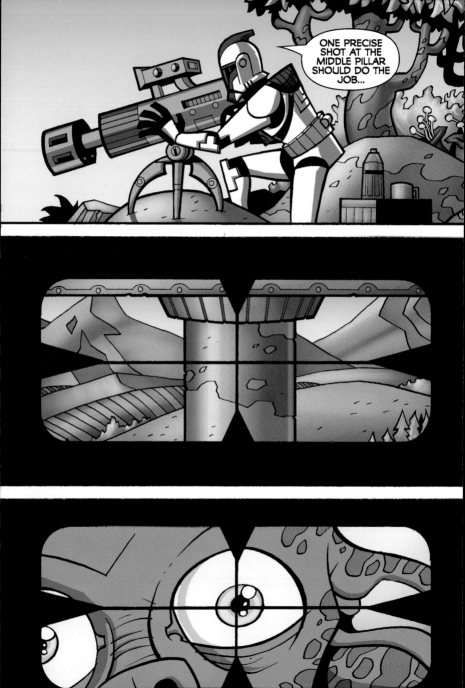

MEEKA MOO GR-GA. *SNIFF. SNIFF.*

MAH-LO DEA?

YOU TWO!

WAIT! GIVE THOSE ROCKETS BACK.

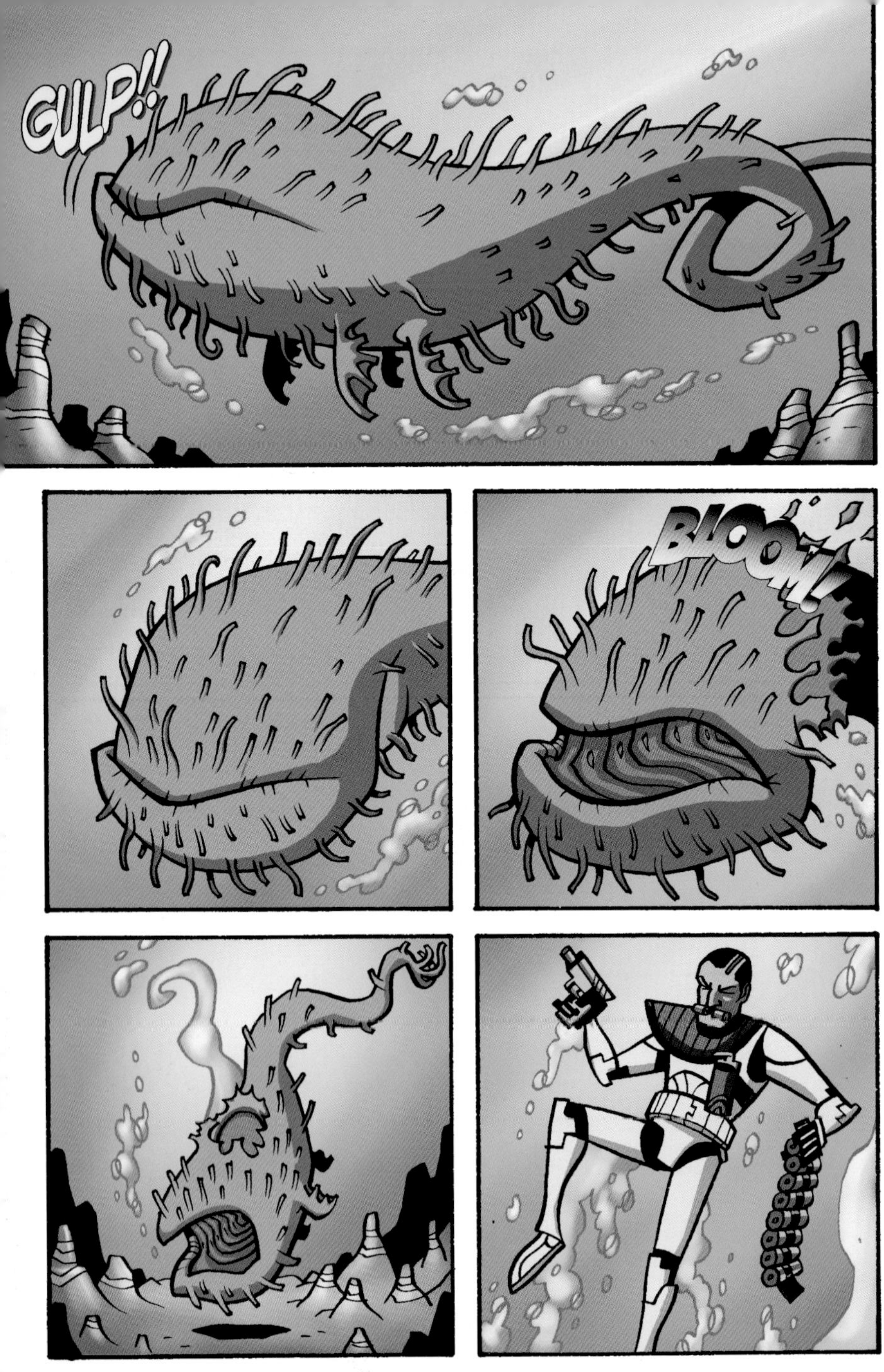
GULP!!
BLOOM!!

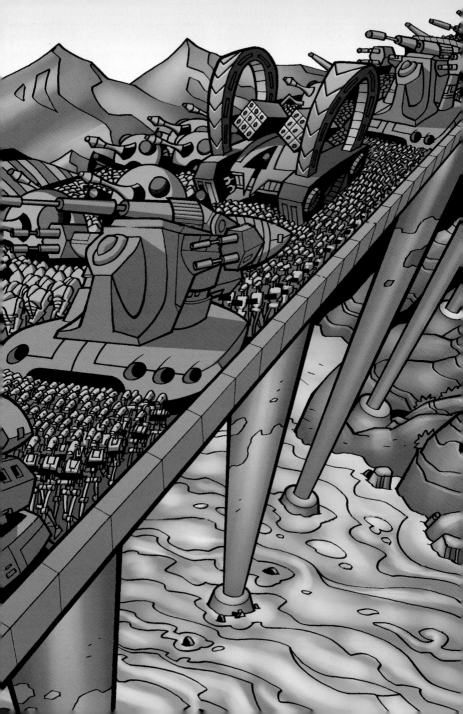

WHAT ARE YOU WAITING FOR? BLOW IT NOW!

WHAT CAN ONE BLASTER DO AGAINST AN ARMY?

WAIT...

...THE ROCKETS!

OKAY. STEADY... STEADY...

KDEW!

MISSION ACCOMPLISHED.

GOOD WORK, POST 473. REPORT BACK TO CAMP -- THERE'S A NEW ASSIGNMENT WAITING FOR YOU.

YES, SIR.